The Haida

JENNIFER NAULT

Weigl

CALGARY
www.weigl.com

Published by Weigl Educational Publishers Limited
6325 10 Street SE
Calgary, Alberta, Canada
T2H 2Z9

Website: www.weigl.com

Library and Archives Canada Cataloguing in Publication Data

Nault, Jennifer
    Haida / Jennifer Nault.

(Canadian Aboriginal art and culture)
Includes index.
ISBN 978-1-55388-329-6 (bound)
ISBN 978-1-55388-330-2 (pbk.)

    1. Haida Indians--Juvenile literature. I. Title. II. Series.
E99.H2N28 2007   j971.1004'9728   C2007-902191-3

Printed in Canada
1 2 3 4 5 6 7 8 9 0 11 10 09 08 07

Project Coordinator Heather Kissock Design Janine Vangool Validator Kwiaahwah Jones, Haida
Gwaii Museum

Photograph credits

Every reasonable effort has been made to trace ownership and to obtain permission to reprint copyright material. The
publishers would be pleased to have any errors or omissions brought to their attention so that they may be corrected in
subsequent printings.

Cover (top left): © Qay'llnagaay Heritage Centre Society; Cover (main): © Canadian Museum of Civilization (VII-B-1836, S92-
4293); © Canadian Museum of Civilization: pages 7 top (VII-B-1075, D2002-002177), 10 (VII-X-783, D2004-26539), 11 right (VII-B-
136a, S85-3277), 12 (VII-X-621, S94-6786), 14 top (VII-B-1543, S93-13420), 14 bottom (VII-B-1128, S2004-1073), 15 top (VII-B-1445,
D2002-000845), 15 bottom (VII-B-364a, D2002-002556), 16 (VII-X-1491, D2004-26644), 17 left (VII-C-2149, S85-3308), 25 (VII-B-1836,
S92-4293), 28 (VII-B-1291, D2002-002223), 29 (VII-B-335, D2002-002343), and 30 (VII-B-2, S85-3269); © Canadian Museum of
Civilization/Robert Davidson: page 27 (VII-B-1822, S89-1738); Courtesy of Christina Craft: page 5; © The Field Museum:
page 9 left (CSA854); Courtesy of Gordon Miller: pages 6, 23; © Qay'llnagaay Heritage Centre Society: pages 8, 11 left,
and 18.

We acknowledge the financial support of the Government of Canada through the Book Publishing Industry Development
Program (BPIDP) for our publishing activities.

Please note

CONTENTS

The People

The Haida have lived in North America for more than 8,000 years. This **First Nations** group lives off the west coast of British Columbia on an **archipelago** called Haida Gwaii. The Haida can also be found in Alaska, on the southern tip of Prince of Wales Island. All Haida speak a distinct language also called Haida.

Archaeological evidence gives clues about the Haida. Their population could have once been as high as 30,000. This is based on the number of sites and settlements discovered around Haida Gwaii. Most of these sites are now abandoned.

Haida Map

This map shows the traditional lands of the Haida in Canada and the United States.

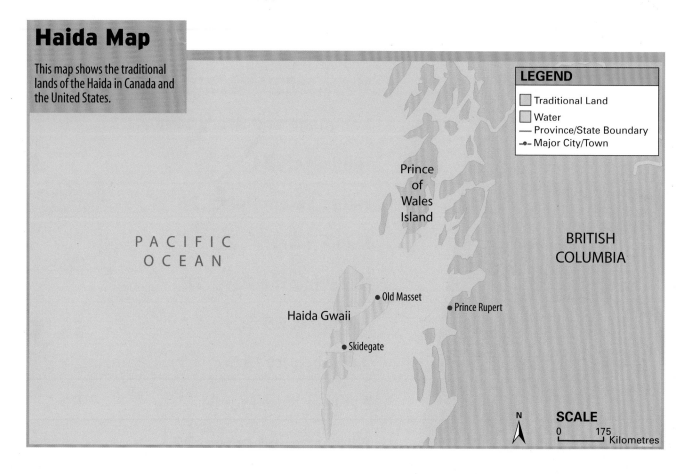

LEGEND
- Traditional Land
- Water
- — Province/State Boundary
- Major City/Town

Prince of Wales Island

BRITISH COLUMBIA

PACIFIC OCEAN

Old Masset

Prince Rupert

Haida Gwaii

Skidegate

N

SCALE
0   175
Kilometres

When European fur traders arrived in the late 1700s, the Haida had about 50 villages scattered throughout Haida Gwaii. The Haida society was highly developed because their island location made it easy to thrive. The climate was warm and lush, and wildlife was abundant, so they had steady access to natural resources such as trees, birds, and fish. As a result, the Haida were excellent hunters and gatherers. Their surroundings provided all they needed to survive.

The Haida lived in large cedar-plank homes called longhouses. They built large and durable canoes from which they fished and hunted sea mammals. Their society was divided into two groups, Ravens and Eagles. Each group had its own resources and **traditions**. The most important Haida ceremony was the **potlatch**.

By 1885, diseases brought by Europeans had reduced the Haida population to 800 people. Despite this terrible loss, the Haida have survived. Today, the Haida population has grown to 4,000. Many Haida have moved away from Haida Gwaii, but those remaining on the islands work in fishing, canning, and logging. Some also work in tourism, showing visitors the beauty and culture of Haida Gwaii.

Much of the Haida **oral** history was lost when their population declined. The Canadian government also prevented the Haida from practising their customs, including the potlatch, for a time. However, Haida culture has flourished again during the past 50 years. Today, Haida art has gained respect around the world.

The Haida have a very close relationship with nature. They believe that all living things are connected and dependent on each other.

Haida Homes

Haida villages had one or more rows of houses lined up along a beach. These were called longhouses. In the middle of the village stood the chief's house, which was larger than the others. The Haida believed that the house was one of the main gifts from Raven, who had stolen the idea from Beaver. This house was the centre of Haida life.

Different regions of Haida Gwaii had slightly different house styles. Haida houses were rectangular and were made of red cedar planks. In the northern part of Haida Gwaii, the houses were framed on the inside. In the south, the frames were on the outside. Thick corner posts supported the huge beams of wood. Typically, the houses were about 30 metres long and 17 metres wide, but some houses could be much larger.

Today, no complete original houses are left on Haida Gwaii. Paintings and historic photos remain to show what the houses looked like. Small models of houses can now be seen in museums.

Some Haida houses had a doorway that featured a **totem pole**. The doorway was created by cutting an opening through the pole. The pole and the front of the house would be artistically carved and painted.

Haida houses had a pitched, or downward sloping, roof. Usually, a Haida house had one fire pit in the centre. There were no windows, so there was a smoke hole through the roof. A board was propped up to protect the opening of the hole from leaks. Smoke from an indoor fire pit would wind its way up and through the hole. An entire household shared the fire for heat and cooking. They slept near the fire on a raised platform. The floor underneath was made of mud that had been dug out to create different levels inside.

The Haida created special tools, such as mauls, to build their houses. Mauls were similar to hammers.

Frontal longhouse poles featured the crests of the family living within.

Haida Communities

The Haida were divided into two social groups. One group was called Raven, and the other was called Eagle. Each group had access to special resources, such as fishing spots and land. Groups also kept their own stories, dances, and songs. Within each group, there were smaller family groups. Marriages could only take place between Eagles and Ravens. Haida in the same group could not marry.

Haida communities spread out over many villages, and each village had several households. A chief was in charge of each household. Most consisted of about 35 people. Some of the more powerful chiefs could command much larger households. A head chief was chosen to control the village itself.

Haida traditions and beliefs are passed down through the generations by senior members of the community.

Haida men often hunted and fished. They sometimes waged war on other First Nations groups of the Northwest Coast. Haida men were known as excellent warriors.

Women in Haida villages were in charge of the home. They performed many of the household chores and kept the community in order. Haida women were accomplished weavers and sewers. They were known for their cedar-bark clothing, head coverings, and basketry.

Haida women wove baskets with spruce roots. After the arrival of Europeans, Haida women made money by selling their creations to settlers and tourists.

GOVERNMENT

The village council of Skidegate is responsible for governing a population of approximately 800.

Today, there are two main Haida villages on Haida Gwaii. One is Skidegate, at the south end of Graham Island. The other village is Masset, at Masset Inlet. Each of these two villages has its own village council. The Council of the Haida Nation governs the two villages. The council was formed in 1980. It was created to protect the land and the rights of the Haida. Part of the Haida **Constitution** says: "Our culture is born of respect, and intimacy with the land and sea and the air around us. We owe our existence to Haida Gwaii."

Haida Clothing

Before they came in contact with Europeans, most Haida wore clothes made of woven strips of red or yellow cedar bark. These strips could be woven to create different kinds of fabrics. Some fabrics were soft, while others were dense and waterproof. The Haida placed crest figures on many articles of clothing. All crest figures related to the two Haida groups, Eagle and Raven.

In the past, capes and other Haida clothing were often decorated with animal symbols, much like totem poles.

Women wore skirts and capes of cedar bark. When the weather was warm, men would wear very little. In cooler weather, they wore long capes of cedar bark. Mountain goat wool was woven into their capes as decoration. Besides woven cedar capes, Haida men also wore large elkskin capes. These were decorated at the sides with paint and fringes. Clothing worn under the capes included leggings, woven aprons, and tunics.

Chiefs wore special clothing, including capes with crest figures. Some capes were lined with sea otter fur. Most importantly, chiefs wore headdresses, often for special ceremonies. Chiefs also wore a carved wooden plaque called a frontlet. It rested on the forehead.

Other people wore headgear as well. Haida women wove hats from spruce roots, which both men and women wore. The broad brims of the hats protected their eyes from the Sun. Men painted the hats, creating animal designs. Colours chosen were mostly red and black, but green and blue were also used.

After contact with Europeans in the late 1700s, Haida clothing began to change. Men and women wore blankets, which they received in exchange for furs. Blankets were wrapped around the body during the day and used to keep warm at night.

Haida clothing today is still adorned with traditional designs and emblems.

MASKS

Haida masks often represented animals, such as marmots. These masks could be used in social dances at a house-warming potlatch.

Among the Haida were several secret societies. Members of these societies had undergone specific **initiation rites** to gain the protection of a powerful guardian spirit. Upon completion of these rites, they were allowed to wear special masks and perform at secret society dances. Secret society dancers would use masks and puppets to represesent wild spirits of the woods. The Haida also wore masks in potlatch performances and at **pole raisings**. Masks were carefully carved and painted, with eyeholes to see through. Some were trimmed with leather and fur, placed to look like facial hair.

Haida Food

Being so close to the Pacific Ocean ensured that food was easy to find. Salmon was a main food source for the Haida. There was no refrigeration, so most of the salmon was smoked. The smoking process involved hanging the fish over a fire so that it would slowly dry and become preserved.

The ocean provided other fish as well, including halibut, cod, smelt, and herring. It also provided whale and seal. All villagers helped in the catching of this food. Haida fishers developed spears, hooks, lines, and nets. Women wove special baskets that were set in the water to trap fish.

On land, the Haida hunted deer, elk, moose, beaver, and other animals. They also picked cranberries, huckleberries, and other plants that were in season. To preserve the berries, the Haida stored them in bottles of whale or seal oil.

Wooden "bent boxes" were sometimes used to cook the food. These boxes were made of bent sheets of cedar bark that were sewn at the corners. The box was filled with water, and red-hot rocks were added for heat. The food was then cooked in the boiling water. Other meat was roasted over open fires.

The Haida stored their food and other items in bentwood boxes. These boxes were often plain, with no decoration. Those that were decorated featured guardian spirits.

RECIPE

Halibut Soup

Ingredients

4 large potatoes

1/2 onion

1 kilogram of halibut, cubed

355 millilitres evaporated milk

1 can cream of celery soup (undiluted)

pepper to taste

water

Equipment

Cutting knife

Cooking pot

Stove

Fork

1. With an adult's help, chop the potatoes and onions, and place them in a pot.

2. Add water to cover the potatoes. Boil until the potatoes are tender.

3. Reduce the heat to medium. Add the halibut, and cook until a fork goes into the fish easily.

4. Add the milk and soup. Simmer for 5 minutes.

5. Add pepper to taste.

Tools, Weapons, and Defence

The Haida were known as strong warriors. Their tough war tactics meant that the Haida were feared by other First Nations groups along the coast, including the Tlingit and the Tsimshian. Battles often took place at sea. To transport themselves, the Haida used their vast supply of giant western red cedar trees to make large canoes. Each canoe was carved from a single cedar tree. Some of these canoes could fit up to 60 paddlers.

Haida warriors were equipped for battle. They wore armour, helmets, and thick war coats. For weapons, they used bows and arrows and spears. Sometimes, heavy stone rings were tied to ropes and hurled at enemy vessels. The stones could then be pulled back and used again. War daggers were also used during both land and sea raids.

Haida war helmets were designed to look like the head of an animal, such as a seal.

Canoes were used not only in war, but for trade and basic travel as well.

HUNTING TOOLS

Haida hunters used different tools and weapons to catch fish and hunt animals. To catch fish, they would use basket traps, rakes, weirs, hooks, lines, and spears. Rakes were large forks made of wood or bone that were fastened to wooden poles. Weirs were fence-like structures that were stretched across a stream. Fish would swim into the weirs and become caught within them. Spears and the bow and arrow were also used. After contact with Europeans, bows and arrows were replaced with firearms.

The Haida used fish hooks and spears to catch halibut, salmon, cod, and other sea life.

Haida Religion

The Haida used nature's resources with respect. They had strong beliefs about the way humans should treat nature and had **rituals** for helping the sick and controlling the weather. In Haida society, shamans, or medicine people, were helped by **supernatural** beings who held special powers. These beings received their powers from aspects of nature, such as the Sun, the Moon, and thunder.

A shaman could be a man or a woman. Male shamans often dealt with trading and warfare. Female shamans often cured illnesses and helped with childbirth. Shamans wore special clothes and jewellery. One important item was a Chilkat, or dancing, blanket, which some shamams wore as a cape during ceremonies. Male shamans would grow their hair long, and some wore an animal bone through their nose.

Chilkat blankets were made from cedar bark and the wool of mountain goats. Their design often featured eagles and ravens.

The Haida believed that everyone had a soul. It was the shaman's responsibility to take care of lost souls. The shaman used a carved, hollow bone called a soul-catcher to capture the lost soul and keep it until it could be returned to its owner. During ceremonies, shamans used other **sacred** items as well. Rattles and charms were used to connect with the spirit world.

Raven rattles usually depict Raven carrying something in his beak. This item symbolizes the Sun. The Haida believe that the Sun was brought to them by Raven.

For the Haida, the spirit world resembled the real world. The spirit world was organized much like their own society. The Haida believed the supernatural beings resided in one of three worlds—the Upper World, or Sky, the Sea, or the Land. Animals were a respected part of the spirit world and held deep **spiritual** meaning. The Haida believed that animals had souls.

The Haida believed that the Upper World was supported by a large pillar that extended up from Haida Gwaii. The Haida themselves lived in Haida Gwaii, the land world. Below Haida Gwaii was the sea world. The entire coastline of British Columbia rested on this world.

Ceremonies and Celebrations

The Haida held several kinds of ceremonies. In their society, high-ranking people organized dance performances, feasts, and potlatches. Potlatches were the most important gathering. It was a time to feast and to display wealth and **social status**. Potlatches were also held to exchange goods. Haida chiefs were at the centre of the potlatches. Chiefs would honour the transfer of a **title** after the death of a noble person. They would also mark the birth of high-ranking children.

People gather to celebrate the completion of a cedar-plank house.

Death was a time to come together as a group. When a noble person died, a **mortuary** potlatch was held. At this event, the title of the deceased was passed on to the heir, usually the next oldest brother. A mortuary totem pole was carved and raised during this ceremony. Next, the belongings of the deceased were given to relatives. Death was not always a sad event. The Haida believed in reincarnation, or that the dead were reborn. People close to death would sometimes choose their next parents.

Completing a cedar-plank house was a reason for celebration. Houses took great effort to build and decorate. The new house owner gave a large potlatch to thank those involved in building the house.

The Haida gathered together to celebrate special events during feasts. Not all feasts were potlatches. Reasons for feasting included death, marriage, or the naming of a newborn. Guests were seated in order of their social status. Special foods were served in feast dishes. The dishes were artistically carved and painted.

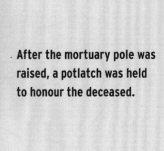

After the mortuary pole was raised, a potlatch was held to honour the deceased.

Music and Dance

Dance has always been an important part of Haida culture. Many dances feature shamans, chiefs, and members of secret societies, but other members of the community dance as well. Dancers wear clothing and masks to represent different characters.

One dance was only performed by men of the Ulala society. A pole that had cedar bark streamers hanging from it would be spun to tell others that the society was about come out from behind the dance curtain. Other important dances were the Eagle Dance, the Raven Dance, and the Salmon Dance.

Dances happened less often by the 1870s. Europeans were frightened by Haida dancing and tried to prevent it. The Haida continued to dance in secret and taught the dances to younger generations so that their traditions would live on.

While masks were often worn during dances, dancers sometimes painted their faces instead.

The Haida made music with drums, rattles, and their voices. Drums could be different sizes, but all had animal skin stretched tightly on a circular wooden frame. Drums were held in one hand. A stick with a leather-padded tip was held in the other hand. It was used to beat the drum. Rattles sometimes took the shape of a raven, so they were called Raven rattles. Usually, the musician used two rattles at one time. They made a swishing sound, which sounded like salmon fins moving through the water. Rattles were used to lure the salmon to Haida villages.

Haida songs told complex stories, often to give thanks. Songs were about love, war, childbirth, death, and dealings with Europeans. Today, the Haida continue to write songs and create dances. These can be experienced through recordings and live performances.

Haida youth are being encouraged to experience the traditional music of their people.

Language and Storytelling

Before Europeans came to the land, the Haida language thrived. Different villages spoke slightly different dialects. Today, three dialects remain. These are the Southern and Northern dialects, both found on Haida Gwaii, and the Kaigani dialect, spoken by Haida who live in Alaska. The biggest difference between dialects is the way that words are pronounced.

The Haida take the survival of their language seriously. People come to the Haida Language House in Skidegate to record and learn the language.

Today, few speakers of the Haida language remain, and most are seniors. The Haida people will lose much of their oral history if they lose their language. Haida in all three dialect regions are working to preserve their language. Senior speakers teach others and make recordings of the language. Teachers are bringing the language back to their students by making it part of lessons. They invite **elders** into their classes to pass along the language through songs and prayer.

Like all cultural groups, the Haida shared knowledge by storytelling. The Haida have different stories to explain **creation** and how the world works.

Raven is one of the most important creatures in Haida myth. Raven is a trickster, but he teaches humans how to live a proper life. One story tells how the first people were born from a huge clamshell on the beach. The people were afraid to leave the shell, but Raven helped them out of the shell so they could live on this earth. Many other stories tell how Raven brought useful items to humans. Raven gave items such as fresh water, salmon, and the house.

In Haida myth, Raven is depicted as a very greedy and mischievous animal, but, through his adventures, he teaches the Haida how to live a good, fulfilling life.

Haida Art

The Haida are well known for their art. Art and decoration were part of everything they created. Art continues to be an important part of Haida culture. The main style of decoration the Haida use is known as flat design. It uses black outlines to create forms and red to fill the spaces inside the lines. Totem poles, masks, and houses all followed this style of decoration.

All Haida items were decorated with spiritual images and crests as well. The crests connected to Haida family heritage. Crests included figures of animals, birds, and sea creatures. Other decorations were attached to supernatural beings. Art showed lessons taught to the Haida by all of these creatures.

Haida flat design remains a popular art form in galleries around the world.

The Haida decorated their clothing, jewellery, tools, canoes, and structures with art. Artistic skills were precise. It took years to learn carving and other artistic skills. Artists worked to improve their abilities all the time. The Haida traded with Europeans and other **Aboriginal** groups for materials and resources they did not have. Through trading, they received mineral **pigments**, stones, and metals, all of which can be found in their art.

Europeans brought new art techniques and materials to the Haida, and the Haida began to experiment with their art styles. They developed art that Europeans preferred and wanted to buy. These items were usually small. Sometimes, the designs differed from the art Haida created for themselves. They created small carvings made of **argillite**, ivory, and silver, as well as wooden and basketry pieces that appealed to European tastes. Many of these items have been collected and saved. Some can be found in museum collections.

Argillite was also used to make dishes. Leaf, berry, and floral patterns were often carved into these dishes.

Haida Totem Poles

Totem poles are huge sculptures carved from giant trees, usually the western red cedar. Poles share a common style with other objects that the Haida carved and painted. The artistry involved in totem pole design developed over thousands of years. Archaeologists have uncovered stone and bone pieces with the same designs from long ago.

The designs on totem poles can mean different things. They may tell of Haida stories, family connections, or important events. Other times, totem poles were carved to celebrate cultural traditions, or used as art. Poles were also used to honour the dead, much like a headstone is used.

The figures commonly found on Haida totem poles include Raven and Eagle. Each figure has its own story to tell and may be carved in different parts of the pole. The larger a figure is, the more important it is to the story.

Haida totem poles were not created to worship the spirit world. They were built as a way to tell stories about the spirits or the Haida community.

MODERN ARTIST

Robert Davidson

Robert Davidson has followed in the tradition of the well-known Haida artist, Bill Reid. When he was only 20 years old, Davidson began an **apprenticeship** with Reid, learning his style and methods. Next, Davidson went to the Emily Carr College of Art and Design in Vancouver to continue studying art. Many call Robert Davidson a new master of the Haida tradition.

Davidson grew up in the Haida community of Masset. He was surrounded by fine carving from a young age. His grandfather was a carver and a chief of the town of Kayung. His father was also a carver, who introduced his children to the craft. Davidson is now one of Canada's most respected artists. He is a master carver of totem poles and masks. He also works as a printmaker, painter, and jeweller.

Davidson carves with both traditional and non-traditional materials. His best-known work is a large bronze sculpture called "Raven Bringing Light to the World." It was created for the Grand Hall at the Canadian Museum of Civilization. It shows a human face that stands for the Sun, the Moon, and the stars. Circling the face is the image of Raven.

Davidson's work is found in a number of important collections. These include the National Gallery of Canada in Ottawa, the Vancouver Art Gallery, the Canadian Museum of Civilization in Gatineau, Quebec, the Southwest Museum in Los Angeles, and the Artists for Kids Gallery in Vancouver. He has also received many honours for his work. In 1995, he received the National Aboriginal Achievement Award for his contribution to First Nations art and culture. He has also received the Order of British Columbia. In 1996, he was awarded the Order of Canada.

"Raven Bringing Light to the World" represents a Haida legend. The legend describes how Raven stole the Sun from an old man who kept it in a tiny box. When Raven stole the Sun, light was brought into the universe.

Studying the Past

Archaeologists study items left by cultures from the past. Some archaeologists have spent time on Haida Gwaii visiting old village sites and examining objects. These Haida sites and **artifacts** give the archaeologists clues about the past.

The first archaeological search on Haida Gwaii, in 1919, produced many clues. Stone tools were found in **intertidal** areas that were once dry land. Old middens, which are hills of litter, were also discovered. These helped the archaeologists learn about the way the Haida once lived and what was important in their lives.

While there is much to still learn, digging around sites must be done carefully. There are many Haida burial areas that should not be disturbed. Today, the Haida are unsure whether the digging should continue.

Archaeologists learn about Haida religion and celebrations by finding musical instruments, including rattles, and other artifacts.

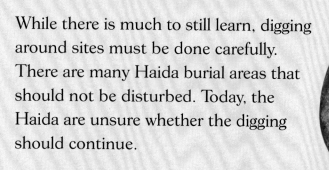

TIMELINE

5,000 years ago
The population of Haida Gwaii is large, with many coastal villages.

1774
Haida Gwaii is visited by Spanish explorer Juan Perez in his ship, *Santiago*.

1787
George Dixon, a British fur trader, meets the Haida and names Haida Gwaii the "Queen Charlotte Islands."

1851
Europeans arrive on Haida Gwaii to obtain gold that is discovered there.

1880
Many ships from England and New England begin visiting the coast, mainly to trade with the Haida.

1884
Changes to the Indian Act stop Haida potlatches until 1951.

1904
Due to disease, mainly smallpox and measles, the population of Haida declines to 800.

1919
The first known archaeological excavation takes place on Haida Gwaii.

2005
The Haida Nation and its neighbours block roads and shut down forestry mills on Haida Gwaii. They do this to protect the forests in their area from being cut down.

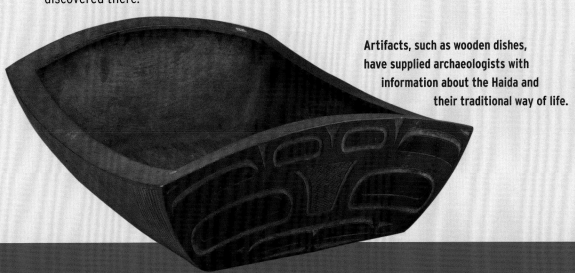

Artifacts, such as wooden dishes, have supplied archaeologists with information about the Haida and their traditional way of life.

Make a Haida Mask

Haida masks were symbols of wild spirits of the woods, which the Haida called *gagiid*. The mouth on the mask was usually frowning. The eyebrows were thick. Small holes were cut for the eyes and mouth. The main colours used to decorate the mask were red and black. Sometimes green and blue were also used. Other decorations included shells, leather, and animal fur.

Materials

computer

construction paper

paint or felt markers, in black, red, blue, and green

scissors

pieces of fur, leather, or shells (optional)

two pieces of string

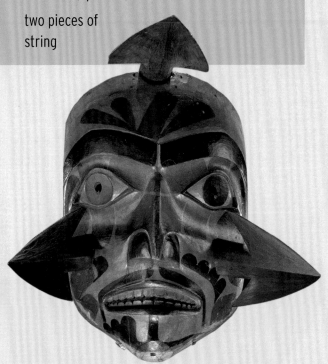

1. Research Haida masks on the internet by typing "Haida" and "mask" into a search engine, such as Google. Pick a mask you would like to make.

2. Cut a large, oval circle out of construction paper. It should be large enough to cover your whole face.

3. Cut holes in the paper for your eyes to look through. Cut a hole for your mouth as well.

4. Colour and decorate your mask.

5. Carefully attach two pieces of string, one on each side of the mask. Tie your mask to your head, and look in the mirror to see yourself.

Further Reading

Haida: Their Art and Culture by Leslie Drew (Big Country Books, 1983) provides interesting information on Haida culture.

There are countless books on Haida Gwaii for people visiting the area. For a visitor's account of Haida Gwaii, read *Haida Gwaii: The Queen Charlotte Islands* by Dennis Horwood and Tom Parkin (Heritage House, 2006).

Websites

Read about the children of Eagle and Raven at the Museum of Civilization. **www.civilization.ca/aborig/haida/haindexe.html**

Visit the Haida village of Skidegate, where you can learn about Haida culture and look at museum artifacts. **www.skidegate.ca**

Learn more about the stories and art of the Haida at **www.virtualmuseum.ca/Exhibitions/ Haida/java/english/art/index.html**.

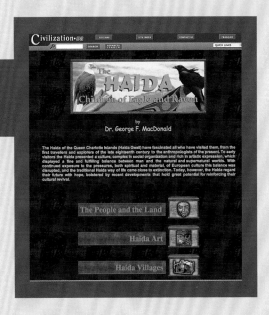

GLOSSARY

Aboriginal: original inhabitants of a country

apprenticeship: the period of time it takes for a person to learn a trade

archaeological: relating to study of ancient societies and the objects they left behind

archipelago: a group of islands

argillite: a soft black rock used in Haida sculpture

artifacts: objects made by humans

constitution: a written record of laws

creation: the forming of the universe and all its inhabitants

elders: the older and more infuential people of a group or community

First Nations: members of Canada's Aboriginal community who are not Inuit or Métis

initiation rites: ceremonies and tasks a person undergoes to be admitted into a group or society

intertidal: beach area that is underwater at high tide

mortuary: relating to burial

oral: spoken, not written

pigments: colouring material used as paint or dye

pole raisings: the placement of totem poles in an upright position after the carving is completed

potlatch: Haida ceremony involving feasting, gift-giving, and dancing

rituals: systems or forms of special ceremonies

sacred: worthy of religious worship

social status: ranking within a community

spiritual: sacred or religious

supernatural: a force existing outside the laws of nature

title: proper name, often giving status

totem pole: a large, upright pole that is carved and painted with First Nations emblems

traditions: established beliefs or practices

INDEX